Yay for Big Brothers!

by Janet Halfmann

illustrated by Shennen Bersani

Kids aren't the only ones who can be Big Brothers. Animals can be Big Brothers, too. Let's peek in on some of them and their families.

I'm a Big Brother Crow. Our family's noisy, hungry chicks beg with mouths open wide. I feed them insects, eggs, mealworms, and maggots. Yum!

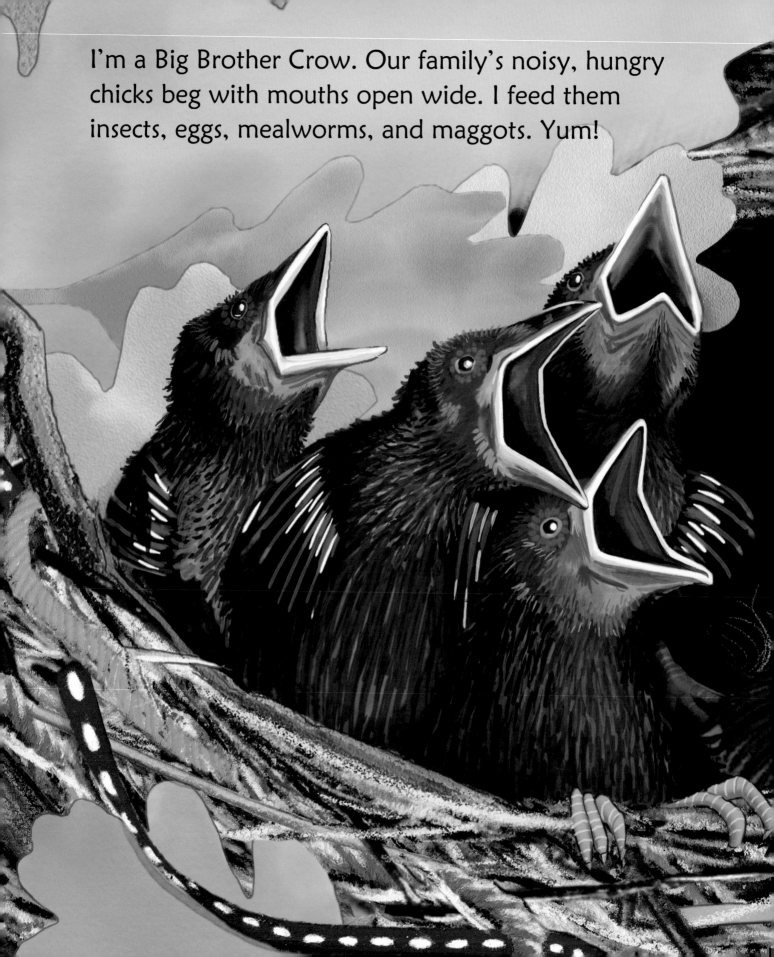

What does the baby in your family eat?

I'm a Big Brother Wolf. My little brother chews on bones and sticks. He thinks my ear is a chew toy, too!

What does the little one in your family like to chew?

I'm a Big Brother Tamarin. The twin infant monkeys in our family can't yet walk. I help carry them through our home in the trees.

How does your little one get around?

I'm a Big Brother Meerkat. Everyone in our big mongoose family is excited to find scorpions. I teach the pups to bite off the stingers before chomping!

Do you teach your little brother or sister new things?

I'm a Big Brother Beaver. The kits in our family get tired when they practice their swimming. I let them hitch a ride on my back.

Does your little one like to play in the water?

I'm a Big Brother Chimpanzee. My little sister chases me around a tree, and I chase her back! What fun!

Do you and your little brother or sister
have fun chasing one another?

I'm a Big Brother Kangaroo. My little brother likes to play-box with me. I'm careful to be gentle.

What games do you and your little one like to play?

I'm a Big Brother Naked Mole Rat. I have lots of little brothers and sisters. Sometimes they wander from the nest in our underground maze of tunnels. It's my job to rescue them.

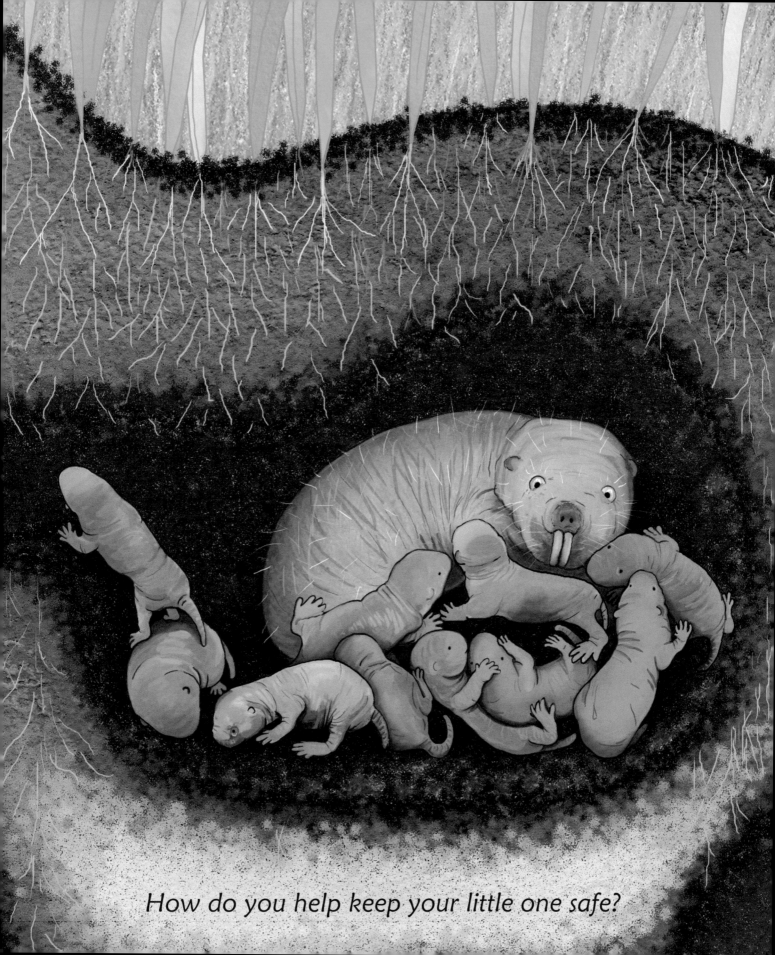

How do you help keep your little one safe?

I'm a Big Brother Dolphin. My little sister has fun with seaweed. We play keep-away and tug-of-war together.

What is your little one's favorite plaything?

I'm a Big Brother African Wild Dog. When my family hunts, I often stay behind and babysit the pups.

Do you sometimes keep your little brother or sister happy when the adults are busy?

I'm a Big Brother Hoary Marmot. I whistle to alert my little brother and sister ground squirrels of danger. They like to give me nose kisses.

Does your little sister or brother like kisses?

Kid Big Brothers do many of the same
things as animal Big Brothers, and more.

Yay for Big Brothers everywhere!

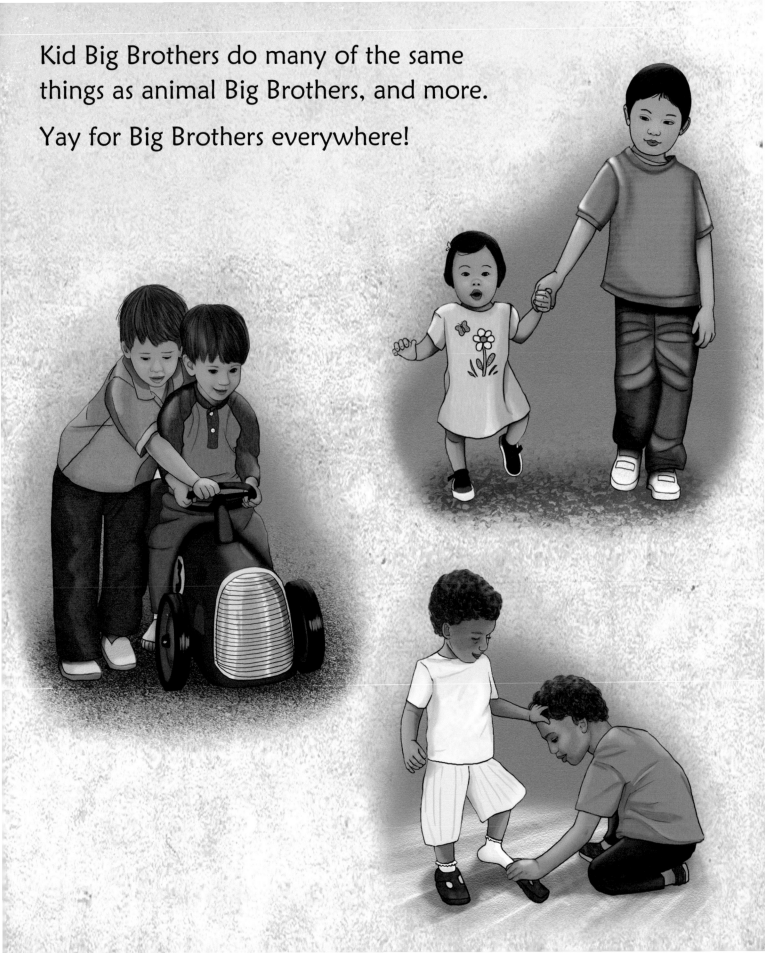

What if an animal could be your Big Brother?
Who would you choose?

For Creative Minds

Glossary

brood	a group of siblings born or hatched at the same time
calves	young dolphins
chicks	young birds
colony	a group of beavers, naked mole rats, or hoary marmots
community	a group of animals that live together in the same area
flock	a group of birds, including crows
infants	young humans, tamarins, and chimpanzees
joeys	young kangaroos
kits	young beavers
mammal	a class of animals with a backbone that has fur (hair); the young drink milk from their mothers
mob	a group of meerkats or kangaroos
offspring	a child or children born to parents
pack	a group of wolves or dogs
pups	young dogs, meerkats, wolves, naked mole rats, or hoary marmots
regurgitate	to bring up food from stomach back into the mouth
siblings	brothers and sisters
troop	a group of chimpanzees

Animal Families That Live In Groups

All of the young animals in this book live in groups. But the groups are very different. Some have only mothers and young. Others have fathers, mothers, brood siblings, and older siblings. Still others include aunts and uncles or unrelated adults.

In addition to living with siblings, which of these animals live with

1. mothers in nursery groups within a large community?

2. mothers and fathers?

3. mothers, fathers, and unrelated adults?

4. mothers of all ages, including grandmothers and daughters about to give birth?

Is your family like any of these animal families? What is your family like?

Beaver kits live with their mothers, fathers, brood siblings, and older siblings.

Chimpanzee infants live in a large troop of males and females of all ages. Mothers form nursery groups within the larger troop to care for the young, while other group members provide protection and search for food.

Dolphin calves spend time in a nursery group that includes expectant mothers and mothers of all ages, including grandmothers. The female dolphins come and go. Older siblings sometimes visit.

Meerkat pups live with their mothers, fathers, brood siblings, and older siblings. The whole mob helps raise the pups.

Tamarin infants live with their mothers, fathers, twin siblings, older siblings, and maybe even a few unrelated adults. The entire group helps raise the infants.

Answers: 1. chimpanzees; 2. beavers, meerkats; 3. tamarins; 4. dolphins

How Many Babies?

Use the chart to answer the questions. The information in the chart is based on averages and what is most common.

	How many babies are born (hatch) at a time?	How much time is normal between babies?
African wild dog	9 to 12 pups	1 year
beaver	3 to 4 kits	1 year
chimpanzee	1 or 2. They can have twins.	5 to 6 years
crow	4 to 6 chicks	1 year
dolphin	1 calf	3 to 6 years
hoary marmot	2 to 5 pups	2 years
kangaroo	1 joey	8 to 12 months
meerkat	3 or 4 pups	4 to 6 months
naked mole rat	12 (up to 27 possible) pups	70 to 80 days
tamarin	1 or 2 with twins most common	1 year
wolf	4 to 6 pups	1 year

1. Which animal has the most babies at the same time?

2. Which animals usually only have one baby at a time?

3. Which two animals might have a baby every six years?

4. Which animal might have pups when the older siblings are about two years old?

5. Which animal usually has two babies at a time (twins)?

6. Which animal mother has the least amount of time between babies?

7. Which animal mother gives birth every eight to twelve months?

8. Which animal gives birth to nine to twelve pups every year?

9. Which animal gives birth to one baby when the older sibling is three to six years old?

Answers: 1. naked mole rat; 2. chimpanzee, dolphin, kangaroo; 3. chimpanzee, dolphin; 4. hoary marmot; 5. tamarin; 6. naked mole rat; 7. kangaroo; 8. African wild dog; 9. dolphin

Fun Facts

Except for the crows (bird), all of the young animals in this book drink milk from their mothers when they are born. That means they are all mammals.

Parents and older siblings spit up food for crow babies to eat: eggs, insects, small vertebrates, plants, and decaying animals.

Wolf pups start eating regurgitated meat when they are about three weeks old. They start hunting when they are six months old.

Beaver kits can swim within twenty-four hours of being born. They will stay with their family until they are about two years old.

Tamarins start eating fruit as early as ten days old. By five weeks, they are eating fruit consistently.

Dolphins swim as soon as they are born. They start to eat fish when they are about three months old.

When kangaroo joeys are about six or seven months old, they lean from their mother's pouch to nibble grass.

A group of chimpanzees is called a community or a troop. It has many families and other groups. There can be up to one hundred fifty chimps in a troop.

With tons of love to my grandsons—Big Brother Desi and Little Brother Sid—my inspirations for this book.—JH
To Big Brother Ryan, honoring his special day with Tracy, October 9, 2021—Love, Mom/SB

Thanks to the following animal experts for verifying the information about the animals:
· Wolves, hoary marmots, beavers, and crows: Naturalists Samantha Blumenkönig & Ute Olsson from Eagle River Nature Center
· Tamarins: Aszya Summers, Curator of Animal Care and Conservation Education at the Racine Zoo
· Meerkats: Educators at Zoo Miami
· Beavers: Cathleen McConnel, Educator at the Point Defiance Zoo & Aquarium
· Chimpanzees: Amy Fultz, Director of Behavior & Research at Chimp Haven
· Naked Mole Rats: Blaine McCarty, Education Operations Coordinator at Zoo Atlanta
· Dolphins: Educators at Clearwater Marine Aquarium

Library of Congress Cataloging-in-Publication Data

Names: Halfmann, Janet, author. | Bersani, Shennen, illustrator.
Title: Yay for big brothers! / by Janet Halfmann ; illustrated by Shennen Bersani.
Description: Mt. Pleasant, SC : Arbordale Publishing, LLC, [2021] | Includes bibliographical references.
Identifiers: LCCN 2021013713 (print) | LCCN 2021013714 (ebook) | ISBN 9781643518220 (paperback) | ISBN 9781643518367 (adobe pdf) | ISBN 9781643518503 (epub) | ISBN 9781643518640 (interactive, dual-language, read-aloud ebook)
Subjects: LCSH: Familial behavior in animals--Juvenile literature. | Brothers--Juvenile literature.
Classification: LCC QL761.5 .H35 2021 (print) | LCC QL761.5 (ebook) | DDC 591.56/3--dc23
LC record available at https://lccn.loc.gov/2021013713
LC ebook record available at https://lccn.loc.gov/2021013714

Bibliography

"2020 Wolf Care Webinars Subscription." Wolf.org, 2013, wolf.org/wolf-info/wild-kids/wolf-families/.
Cawthon Lang, K.A. "Primate Factsheets: Cotton-top Tamarin: Behavior," 18 May 2005. National Primate Research Center Library at the University of Wisconsin-Madison.
"Conservation Expedition." Canisius College, 17 May 2014, www.canisius.edu/about/news-and-events/news/conservation-expedition.
Cutchins, Judy, and Ginny Johnston. *Parenting Papas : Unusual Animal Fathers.* New York, Morrow Junior Books, 1994.
"Do Animals Teach?" National Wildlife Federation, www.nwf.org/Magazines/National-Wildlife/2015/OctNov/Animals/Animal-Teaching.
Gunderman, Danielle. "Marmota Caligata (Hoary Marmot)." Animal Diversity Web, animaldiversity.org/accounts/Marmota_caligata/.
"Hoary Marmot." Animal Spot, 20 Oct. 2011, www.animalspot.net/hoary-marmot.html.
Hoskyns, Robin. "Scorpions." Kalahari Blog, 12 Sept. 2013, kalahariblog.wordpress.com/2013/09/12/scorpions/.
Jarrow, Gail, and Paul W. Sherman. *Animal Baby Sitters.* New York, Franklin Watts, 2001.
Kuczaj, Stan A., and Holli C. Eskelinen. "Why Do Dolphins Play?" *Animal Behavior and Cognition*, vol. 2, no. 2, 2014, p. 113, 10.12966/abc.05.03.2014.
Masson, J. Moussaieff. *The Evolution of Fatherhood : A Celebration of Animal and Human Families.* New York, Ballantine Books, 2001.
"Naked Mole-Rat." Smithsonian's National Zoo, 25 Apr. 2016, nationalzoo.si.edu/animals/naked-mole-rat.
Packard, Jane. "Wolf Behavior." *Wolves: Behavior, Ecology, and Conservation*, edited by L. David Mech. Chicago, University Of Chicago Press, 2003.
Pringle, Laurence, and Bob Marstall. *Crows! : Strange and Wonderful.* Honesdale, Pa., Boyds Mills Press, 2002.
Ryden, Hope. *Joey : The Story of a Baby Kangaroo.* New York, Tambourine Books, 1994.
Ryden, Hope. *Lily Pond : Four Years with a Family of Beavers.* New York, N.Y., Lyons & Burford, Publishers, 1997.
Ryden, Hope. *The Beaver.* New York, Lyons & Burford, 1992.
Savage, Candace. *Mother Nature : Animal Parents and Their Young.* Vancouver ; Toronto, Greystone Books, 1997.
Sherman, Paul W., et al. *The Biology of the Naked Mole-Rat.* Princeton, Princeton University Press, 2017.
Strong, Paul. *Beavers : Where Waters Run.* Econo-Clad Books, 2001.
"The Young and the Restless: Watching Neighborhood Crows." All about Birds, 15 Jan. 2010, www.allaboutbirds.org/news/the-young-and-the-restless-watching-neighborhood-crows/.
Weaver, Melina. Answer from "Ask a Biologist" to my question about what older siblings feed baby crows, 26 July 2018. E-mail.
"Wild Meerkats School Their Young." University of Cambridge, 14 July 2006, www.cam.ac.uk/research/news/wild-meerkats-school-their-young.

Lexile Level: AD520L

Text Copyright 2021 © by Janet Halfmann
Illustration Copyright 2021 © by Shennen Bersani

The "For Creative Minds" educational section may be copied by the owner for personal use or by educators using copies in classroom settings.

Printed in the US
This product conforms to CPSIA 2008
First Printing

Arbordale Publishing, LLC
Mt. Pleasant, SC 29464
www.ArbordalePublishing.com